S·E·C Girls' business®

Written by
Fay Angelo, Heather Anderson and Rose Stewart

Illustrated by Julie Davey

This book is about important girls' business.

In this book, you can find out about:

Body Changes
on pages 4–7
& page 14

Periods
on pages 15–25

Breasts
on pages 12 & 13

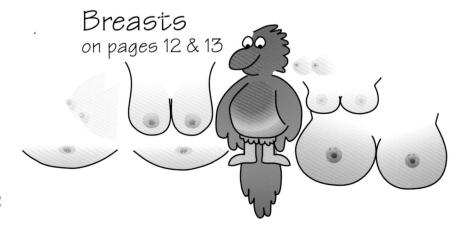

Puberty

getting taller

Growing up

Mums, dads, carers and teachers can find out useful things also.

People grow

all through ...

What's hot & what's not

JUST STARTING

4

and change

their lives

5

Puberty is when your body gradually changes

In your life, there are times

from the body of a child

to the body

Where do you fit

6

Journey

when your body changes a lot.

on this journey?

About puberty

Puberty changes
the way our bodies
look and work,
and the way
we think
and feel.

It prepares a girl's body for having a baby
some time in the future, if she chooses.

If you want to know more
about how babies are made,
you could talk to an adult you trust.

When will it happen?

Puberty can happen
earlier for some
and
later
for
others.

When your body is
the right size and shape for you
it will begin to change.

Some people begin puberty as young as 8
while others may not start until 16.

It's OK if you change earlier
... or later.

Your body will do what is right for you.

9

Girls

Breasts develop.
Vaginal discharge (wet white stuff).
The ovaries ripen a tiny egg each month.
Periods begin.

> Hey, I've grown taller, I'm hungrier,
> I've got pimples, I've got body hair,
> hair under my arms and I've got pubic hair.

> Me too!

Inside the body

ovaries

uterus

vagina

happen during puberty

Body

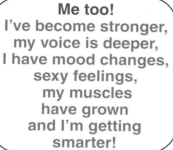

Me too!
I've become stronger,
my voice is deeper,
I have mood changes,
sexy feelings,
my muscles
have grown
and I'm getting
smarter!

Cool.

Boys

Voice breaks.
Testicles make sperm.
Wet dreams — (when sperm
comes out of the penis
during sleep).

pubic hair

penis

testicle

11

Special Girls' Business

Breasts come in all shapes and siz**es**.

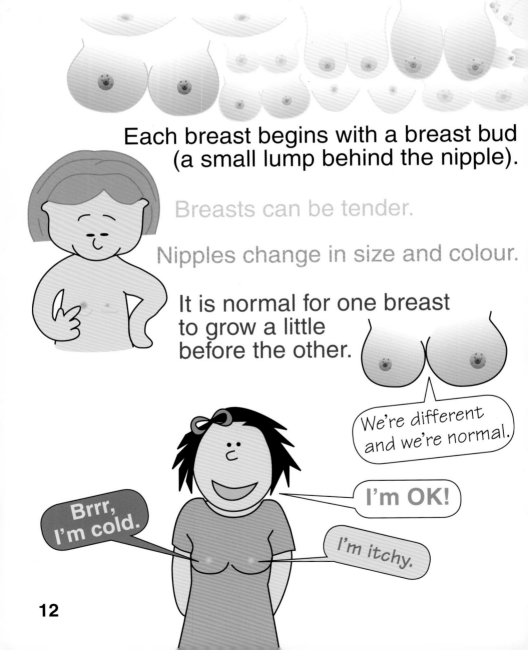

Each breast begins with a breast bud (a small lump behind the nipple).

Breasts can be tender.

Nipples change in size and colour.

It is normal for one breast to grow a little before the other.

We're different and we're normal.

Brrr, I'm cold.

I'm OK!

I'm itchy.

Breasts like support whether they are big or little.

Crop tops, camis, bras and sports bras are the answer.

Some girls can feel shy and embarrassed about their new shape...

while others are OK about it.

Whatever your new shape is, feel proud of it.

13

Early Signs of Puberty

Hey, some
extra HAIR.

And now some
MORE HAIR.

Oh, what's this LUM
doing here?

*And now, what's this
white stuff on my undies?*

The wet white stuff
(vaginal discharge)
comes out of the vagina.
Sometimes you'll see a
small amount on your undies.
It is normal to have
vaginal discharge
from puberty onwards.

It is a sign that periods will start
in several months.

Periods

What is a period?

It is a small amount
of blood which comes
out of the vagina
each month.

When will it happen?

Some girls get their
period as young as
8 years old, other girls
may be as old as 16
before theirs begin.

Why do girls have periods?

Inside your body you have a uterus.

This is the place where a baby can grow.

Every month the uterus makes a special lining of blood.
This is to feed and protect a baby if one is made.

When a baby is not made, the blood dribbles slowly out of the vagina.

Once the blood has all come out, the period stops.

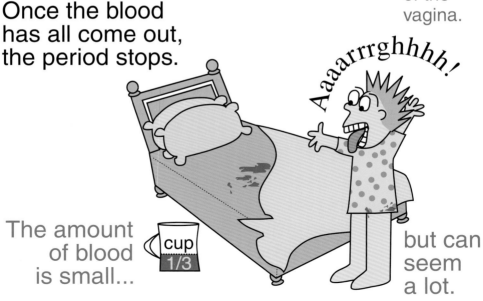

Aaaarrrghhhh!

The amount of blood is small...

cup 1/3

but can seem a lot.

A period usually lasts 3–7 days.

Usually you will have a period each month.

When you first start having periods they may not happen each month and this is OK.

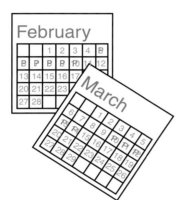

If you are worried about how often you have a period, talk to your parent, carer or doctor.

How will you know when you get your period?

A feeling of wetness around your vagina.
A small amount of blood on your undies.

You will notice the blood is a different colour from day to day.

How will you feel around the time of your period?

You may have mood swings.

Happy, sad, laughing, shy, silly, teary, etc. Sometimes a little grumpy.

A need for more privacy.

A need for extra cuddles.

Maybe some pain in your tummy.

Breasts may be tender.

What can help?

Doing
interesting
things.

A hot water bottle
or heat bag
on the tummy.

Aahh...

Talk to Mum, Dad
a teacher or a friend
about your feelings.

Will I
ever feel
normal
again?

Sometimes tablets from
the chemist or doctor.

When your period starts, what do you need?

A period pad to catch the blood.

A pad has a sticky strip

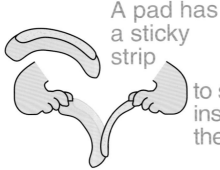

to stick inside the undies.

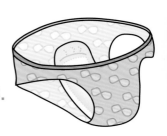

On the last day of your period you could use a panty liner.

Pads come in different shapes and sizes – you might want to check out which is best for you.

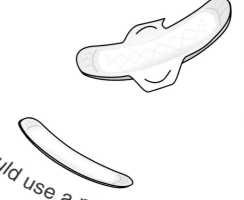

About using pads

Pads need changing often.
Some girls change every time
they go to the toilet.

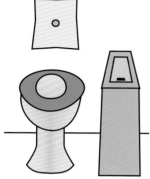

If you wear a pad
for more than 3 hours
it can start to smell.

Used pads should be
wrapped and
put in the bin.

Pads can't be
flushed down
the toilet.

Wash
hands
before
and after
changing

It is normal for blood
to sometimes go on
the undies or sheets.

If you have blood on your clothing or on your
sheet, soak it in cold water – then wash.

21

About tampons

Some girls use a tampon.

A tampon is about this size
and can be carried in your pocket.

The tampon goes into the vagina
and soaks up the blood.

Bowel

Uterus

It
goes
in like
this.

Bladder Vagina

Tampons can be great for
sport and swimming.

Some tampons have
an applicator to help
you put them in.

At first you may need help
and practice, as it can be tricky.

You can buy different sized tampons to suit
the blood flow.

How to use a tampon

You must always **wash your hands carefully** before and after using tampons.

Remove the wrapper

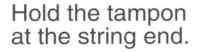

Hold the tampon at the string end.

Lie on the bed, squat or stand with one foot on the toilet.

Insert the rounded end in first and gently push it right in.

To remove the tampon, gently pull out with the string.

Tampons need to be changed about every 4 hours

Getting ready

It is a good idea to get ready
before your period starts.

You could make a kit.
Ask the person who cares for you to help.

You could use:
a groovy
make up purse,
a zipped pencil case,
a drawstring bag,
or another fun idea.

Put in:
- 2 pads
- 2 paper bags
- spare undies
- plastic bag (for used undies)
- disposable wipes.

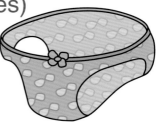

Pads and tampons can be bought at:

- the supermarket
- the chemist

- the corner shop
- the milk bar

- in some toilets
- the service station.

Mum, Dad or whoever cares for you will buy some when they do the shopping.

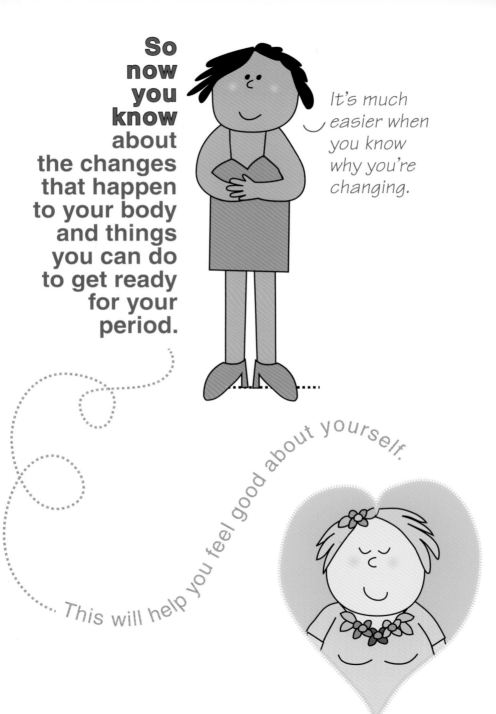

So now you know about the changes that happen to your body and things you can do to get ready for your period.

It's much easier when you know why you're changing.

This will help you feel good about yourself.

Secret Girls' Business® *is part of your exciting life's journey.*

So now you know ...

In the next few pages there are hints for Mums, Dads, carers and teachers.

HANDY HINTS FOR MUMS, DADS AND CARERS

Read through the book, *Secret Girls' Business*® a few times – becoming comfortable and familiar with the terminology and explanations.

It's helpful for girls to have access to correct information so they feel OK about their body changes. A positive attitude towards growth and change will empower girls to become confident young women.

Your reaction to your child's changes and questions will have a long lasting impression on your child's confidence and self-esteem.

Parents need to be responsive to questions. If you feel uneasy answering questions it's OK to acknowledge this feeling.

Parents need to be prepared for discussion at any time. Sexuality education is an ongoing process – it can be part of everyday communication and does not have to be a 'formal' talk or a 'one off chat'.

It's OK to share past (& present) experiences in a positive way.

Convey the message to girls that discussion about body changes and periods is private. Let them know which people they can talk to about these issues.

Be aware and sensitive that girls may have mood changes associated with their menstrual cycle.

Ensure there are always pads in the house (especially before the first period).

More Secret Girls' Business® provides additional information for girls as they experience puberty.

SPECIALLY FOR DADS AND IMPORTANT MALES IN YOUR LIFE

Men can support girls by:

> reading and discussing the book

> when planning trips in the car, allow regular toilet stops, so pads or tampons can be changed

> helping other siblings, including brothers, to understand about periods

> encouraging brothers to be respectful and understanding

> being prepared to include pads or tampons in the shopping basket

> being aware that girls may be teary, over-sensitive and out of sorts – back off and be a bit gentle when girls are like this.

Dad, I think it's time we had a little talk.

It helps if teachers:

read about puberty, and the needs of young people going through this change

think about how to incorporate sexuality education in the school (a recent British survey showed 1 in 6 girls are entering puberty by the age of 8 years old)

make sanitary bins available in toilets for girls of all ages

have books in the classroom and the library on puberty suitable for children of all ages

don't assume that all girls have the knowledge and skills to use pads and tampons, they may require further information or assistance

Let girls know:

if they need help, they can talk to any teacher they feel comfortable with – it doesn't have to be their particular grade teacher

where pads are kept in the school

that pads are taken on all excursions and camps.

Additional resources:

A poster set is available with teaching discussion notes to support a comprehensive sexuality program (see www.secretgb.com).

NB *More Secret Girls' Business®* provides more comprehensive information for girls as they experience puberty.

AND TEACHERS

Things to consider:

- Lessons, teaching blocks, swimming, sport, long trips, and camps can present difficulties for girls who have their period. This should be an important focus when planning activities.

- Girls can be caught unawares with periods – it is helpful if schools and individual teachers plan how they will deal with these situations.

- If a girl asks for a pad – give 2 more to last the day

- Be aware that girls may have mood changes associated with their menstrual cycle

– they may be

teary,

over-sensitive

and

out
of
sorts.

Books written and published by

Secret Girls' Business®

Please visit us at www.secretgb.com or email at secretgb@hotmail.com